Electric Smoker Cookbook

By Brad Hoskinson

Table of Contents

Smoked Maple-Glazed Salmon 6

Electric Smoker BBQ Ribs 8

Applewood-Smoked Pork Butt 10

Hickory-Smoked Brisket 12

Smoked Garlic and Herb Chicken 14

Mesquite-Smoked Turkey Breast 16

Cherrywood-Smoked Pork Chops 18

Smoked Sausage Platter 20

Smoked Mac and Cheese 21

Smoked Paprika Shrimp Skewers 23

Smoked Teriyaki Tofu 25

Pecan-Smoked Ribeye Steak 27

Cedar-Plank Smoked Trout 29

Smoked Vegetarian Chili 31

Smoked Stuffed Bell Peppers 33

Smoked Pineapple Salsa 35

Smoked Onion and Mushroom Soup 37

Smoked Gouda and Bacon Dip 39

Smoked Artichoke Hearts 41

Smoked Portobello Mushrooms 43

Smoked Cheddar and Beer Soup 45

Smoked Sweet Potato Fries 47

Smoked Garlic Hummus 49

Smoked Avocado Guacamole... 51

Smoked Mango Salsa 53

Smoked Eggplant Baba Ganoush... 55

Smoked Corn on the Cob 57

Smoked Cabbage Steaks 58

Smoked Brussels Sprouts with Bacon.................................. 60

Smoked Asparagus Bundles 62

Smoked Tomato and Basil Salad 64

Smoked Caprese Skewers 66

Smoked Watermelon Salad... 68

Smoked Peach Cobbler 70

Smoked Blueberry Pie... 72

Smoked Chocolate Brownies.. 74

Smoked Pecan Pie.. 76

Smoked Pineapple Upside-Down Cake................................. 78

Smoked Banana Bread 80

Smoked Apple Crisp 82

Smoked Cherry Cobbler 84

Smoked Almond Butter Cookies 86

Smoked Coconut Macaroons 88

Smoked Lemon Pound Cake... 90

Smoked Pistachio Biscotti 92

Smoked Cranberry Orange Muffins...................................... 94

Smoked Vanilla Bean Ice Cream... 96

Smoked Espresso Tiramisu... 98

Smoked Bourbon Pecan Pie 101

Smoked Raspberry Cheesecake 103

Smoked Maple-Glazed Salmon

Smoked Maple-Glazed Salmon is a delightful dish that combines salmon's rich, smoky flavor with a sweet and savory maple glaze. It's perfect for a special occasion or any time you want to impress your guests.

Prep Time:15 minutes

Ingredients:

- ✓ 4 salmon fillets (6-8 ounces each)
- ✓ 1/2 cup pure maple syrup
- ✓ 2 tablespoons Dijon mustard
- ✓ 2 tablespoons soy sauce
- ✓ 1 teaspoon minced garlic
- ✓ 1 teaspoon smoked paprika
- ✓ Salt and black pepper to taste
- ✓ Wood chips for smoking (e.g., applewood or hickory)

Method:

1. Whisk together the maple syrup, Dijon mustard, soy sauce, minced garlic, smoked paprika, salt, and black pepper in a small bowl to create the glaze.
2. Preheat your smoker to 225°F (110°C) using the wood chips for flavor.
3. Pat the salmon fillets dry with paper towels and place them on a baking sheet. Brush each fillet generously with the maple glaze, reserving some for later basting.

4. Place the salmon fillets on the smoker grate and close the lid. Smoke for approximately 1-1.5 hours or until the salmon reaches an internal temperature of 145°F (63°C).
5. Periodically baste the salmon with the reserved maple glaze while smoking.
6. Once done, remove the smoked maple-glazed salmon from the smoker and let it rest for a few minutes before serving. Enjoy your delicious smoked salmon!

Electric Smoker BBQ Ribs

Electric Smoker BBQ Ribs are tender, juicy, and packed with smoky barbecue flavor. This recipe is a crowd-pleaser, and an electric smoker makes it easy and convenient.

Prep Time:15 minutes

Ingredients:

- ✓ 2 racks of baby back ribs
- ✓ 1/4 cup brown sugar
- ✓ 2 tablespoons paprika
- ✓ 2 teaspoons salt
- ✓ 1 teaspoon black pepper
- ✓ 1 teaspoon garlic powder
- ✓ 1 teaspoon onion powder
- ✓ 1/2 teaspoon cayenne pepper (adjust for heat preference)
- ✓ Your favorite BBQ sauce

Method:

1. Remove the membrane from the back of the ribs for tenderness. Use a butter knife to loosen it and then pull it off.
2. Mix the brown sugar, paprika, salt, black pepper, garlic powder, onion powder, and cayenne pepper to create a dry rub.
3. Rub the dry spice mixture generously over both sides of the ribs, ensuring they are well coated. Let them sit at

room temperature for about 30 minutes to allow the flavors to meld.

4. Preheat your electric smoker to 225°F (110°C) using the wood chips you choose (hickory or applewood work well).

5. Place the seasoned ribs in the smoker, bone down, and smoke for approximately 4-5 hours or until the meat is tender. You can periodically baste the ribs with your favorite BBQ sauce during the last hour of smoking.

6. Once done, remove the smoked BBQ ribs from the smoker, slice them, and serve with extra BBQ sauce. Enjoy!

Applewood-Smoked Pork Butt

Applewood-Smoked Pork Butt is a classic barbecue favorite that's tender and full of smoky goodness. This recipe requires patience but yields incredible results.

Prep Time:15 minutes

Ingredients:

- ✓ 1 pork butt (7-9 pounds)
- ✓ 1/4 cup yellow mustard
- ✓ 1/4 cup apple cider vinegar
- ✓ Your favorite pork rub
- ✓ Applewood chunks or chips for smoking

Method:

1. Trim any excess fat from the pork butt and apply a thin layer of yellow mustard all over the surface as a binder.
2. Season the pork butt generously with your favorite pork rub, making sure to coat it evenly. Wrap the seasoned meat in plastic wrap and refrigerate for at least 2 hours or overnight for better flavor penetration.
3. Preheat your smoker to 225°F (110°C) using applewood chunks or chips for smoke flavor.
4. Place the seasoned pork butt on the smoker grate, fat side up, and insert a meat thermometer into the thickest part of the meat without touching the bone.
5. Smoke the pork butt for approximately 1.5 hours per pound or until the internal temperature reaches around 200°F (93°C).

6. Once done, remove the applewood-smoked pork butt from the smoker and let it rest for 30 minutes before pulling the meat apart using two forks. Serve with your favorite barbecue sauce and sides. Enjoy!

Hickory-Smoked Brisket

Hickory-Smoked Brisket is a true barbecue masterpiece known for its smoky, tender, and flavorful meat. It takes time and patience but is well worth the effort.

Prep Time:15 minutes

Ingredients:

- ✓ 1 whole beef brisket (10-12 pounds)
- ✓ 1/4 cup yellow mustard
- ✓ Your favorite beef brisket rub
- ✓ Hickory wood chunks or chips for smoking

Method:

1. Trim excess fat from the Brisket, leaving about 1/4 inch of fat on the surface. Apply a thin layer of yellow mustard as a binder.
2. Season the Brisket with your chosen beef brisket rub, ensuring even coverage. Wrap the Brisket in plastic wrap and refrigerate for at least 2 hours or overnight for enhanced flavor.
3. Preheat your smoker to 225°F (110°C) using hickory wood chunks or chips for that classic smoky flavor.
4. Place the seasoned Brisket on the smoker grate, fat side up, and insert a meat thermometer into the thickest part of the meat without touching the bone.
5. Smoke the Brisket for approximately 1.5 hours per pound or until the internal temperature reaches around

195-205°F (90-96°C). The meat should be tender and have a nice bark.

6. Once done, remove the hickory-smoked Brisket from the smoker and let it rest for at least 30 minutes before slicing it thinly against the grain. Serve with your favorite barbecue sauce, or enjoy it as is. Savor the smoky goodness!

Smoked Garlic and Herb Chicken

Smoked Garlic and Herb Chicken is a flavorful and aromatic dish perfect for a backyard barbecue. The combination of herbs and smoky flavors makes this chicken a crowd-pleaser.

Prep Time:15 minutes

Ingredients:

- ✓ 4 bone-in, skin-on chicken breasts
- ✓ 4 cloves garlic, minced
- ✓ 2 tablespoons fresh rosemary, chopped
- ✓ 2 tablespoons fresh thyme, chopped
- ✓ 2 tablespoons fresh parsley, chopped
- ✓ 2 tablespoons olive oil
- ✓ Salt and black pepper to taste
- ✓ Wood chips for smoking (e.g., cherry or pecan)

Method:

1. Combine the minced garlic, chopped rosemary, thyme, parsley, olive oil, salt, and black pepper in a small bowl to create a herb and garlic paste.
2. Loosen the skin on each chicken breast and rub the herb and garlic paste evenly under the skin.
3. Preheat your smoker to 275°F (135°C) using the wood chips for smoke flavor.
4. Place the chicken breasts on the smoker grate, skin side up.

5. Smoke the chicken for approximately 1.5 to 2 hours or until the internal temperature reaches 165°F (74°C) and the skin is crispy.
6. Once done, remove the smoked garlic and herb chicken from the smoker and let it rest for a few minutes before serving. The flavorful herb and smoky aroma make this dish a hit at any gathering. Enjoy!

Mesquite-Smoked Turkey Breast

Mesquite-smoked turkey Breast is a delicious and healthier alternative to a whole-smoked turkey. The smoky, flavorful meat pairs perfectly with various side dishes and is great for sandwiches, too.

Prep Time:15 minutes

Ingredients:

- ✓ 1 boneless turkey breast (about 2-3 pounds)
- ✓ 1/4 cup olive oil
- ✓ 2 tablespoons mesquite wood chips (soaked in water for 30 minutes)
- ✓ 2 teaspoons garlic powder
- ✓ 2 teaspoons onion powder
- ✓ 1 teaspoon smoked paprika
- ✓ 1 teaspoon dried thyme
- ✓ Salt and black pepper to taste

Method:

1. Mix the olive oil, garlic powder, onion powder, smoked paprika, dried thyme, salt, and black pepper in a small bowl to create a marinade.
2. Place the turkey breast in a resealable plastic bag or shallow dish and pour the marinade over it. Seal the bag or cover the dish and refrigerate for at least 2 hours or overnight for maximum flavor.
3. Preheat your smoker to 275°F (135°C) and add the soaked mesquite wood chips for smoke.

4. Remove the turkey breast from the marinade and let any excess drip off. Place it on the smoker grate.
5. Smoke the turkey breast for approximately 2-3 hours or until it reaches an internal temperature of 165°F (74°C).
6. Once done, remove the mesquite-smoked turkey breast from the smoker and let it rest for 10-15 minutes before slicing. Serve as a main dish with your favorite sides, or use it for sandwiches. Enjoy!

Cherrywood-Smoked Pork Chops

Cherrywood-Smoked Pork Chops are a delightful treat for pork lovers. The sweet and fruity aroma of cherrywood smoke complements the savory pork chops beautifully.

Prep Time:15 minutes

Ingredients:

- ✓ 4 bone-in pork chops (1 inch thick)
- ✓ 2 tablespoons olive oil
- ✓ 2 teaspoons smoked paprika
- ✓ 2 teaspoons garlic powder
- ✓ 2 teaspoons brown sugar
- ✓ 1 teaspoon salt
- ✓ 1/2 teaspoon black pepper
- ✓ Cherrywood chips for smoking (soaked in water for 30 minutes)

Method:

1. Combine the olive oil, smoked paprika, garlic powder, brown sugar, salt, and black pepper in a small bowl to create a spice rub.
2. Rub the spice mixture evenly over both sides of the pork chops.
3. Preheat your smoker to 225°F (110°C) and add the soaked cherrywood chips for smoke flavor.
4. Place the seasoned pork chops on the smoker grate.

5. Smoke the pork chops for approximately 1.5 to 2 hours or until they reach an internal temperature of 145°F (63°C).
6. Once done, remove the cherrywood-smoked pork chops from the smoker and let them rest for a few minutes before serving. Serve with your favorite sides for a delightful meal. Enjoy!

Smoked Sausage Platter

A Smoked Sausage Platter is a crowd-pleasing appetizer or snack perfect for parties and gatherings. The smoky sausages pair well with a variety of dipping sauces.

Prep Time:15 minutes

Ingredients:

- ✓ 1 pound smoked sausages (such as kielbasa or andouille)
- ✓ 1 tablespoon olive oil
- ✓ Your favorite dipping sauces (e.g., barbecue sauce, mustard, ranch)

Method:

1. Preheat your smoker to 225°F (110°C).
2. Brush the smoked sausages with olive oil to avoid sticking to the smoker grate.
3. Place the sausages on the smoker grate.
4. Smoke the sausages for approximately 1-1.5 hours or until they are heated and have a smoky flavor.
5. Once done, remove the smoked sausages from the smoker and serve them on a platter with your favorite dipping sauces. Enjoy your Smoked Sausage Platter!

Smoked Mac and Cheese

Smoked Mac and Cheese is a delightful twist on the classic comfort food. The smoky flavor takes this dish to a whole new level of deliciousness.

Prep Time:15 minutes

Ingredients:

✓ 1 pound elbow macaroni
✓ 4 cups shredded cheddar cheese
✓ 2 cups milk
✓ 1/4 cup unsalted butter
✓ 2 teaspoons smoked paprika
✓ 1 teaspoon garlic powder
✓ Salt and black pepper to taste
✓ Wood chips for smoking (e.g., applewood or hickory)

Method:

✓ Cook the elbow macaroni according to the package instructions until al dente. Drain and set aside.
✓ In a large saucepan, melt the unsalted butter over medium heat. Stir in the smoked paprika and garlic powder.
✓ Gradually add the milk while stirring, then add the shredded cheddar cheese. Stir until the cheese is fully melted and the sauce is smooth.
✓ Season the cheese sauce with salt and black pepper to taste.

✓ Combine the cooked macaroni with the cheese sauce in a large mixing bowl, ensuring the pasta is evenly coated.

✓ Preheat your smoker to 225°F (110°C) using the wood chips you choose for smoke flavor.

✓ Transfer the mac and cheese mixture to a heatproof dish or aluminum pan suitable for smoking.

✓ Place the dish on the smoker grate and smoke for approximately 30-45 minutes or until the mac and cheese develops a smoky flavor.

✓ Once done, remove the smoked mac and cheese from the smoker and let it cool for a few minutes before serving. Enjoy the rich, smoky goodness!

Smoked Paprika Shrimp Skewers

Smoked Paprika Shrimp Skewers are a quick and flavorful dish for grilling or smoking. The smoky paprika adds a unique depth of flavor to the succulent shrimp.

Prep Time:15 minutes

Ingredients:

- ✓ 1 pound large shrimp, peeled and deveined
- ✓ 2 tablespoons olive oil
- ✓ 2 teaspoons smoked paprika
- ✓ 1 teaspoon garlic powder
- ✓ 1/2 teaspoon onion powder
- ✓ 1/2 teaspoon cayenne pepper (adjust for heat preference)
- ✓ Salt and black pepper to taste
- ✓ Wood skewers (soaked in water for 30 minutes)

Method:

1. Whisk together the olive oil, smoked paprika, garlic powder, onion powder, cayenne pepper, salt, and black pepper to create a marinade.
2. Thread the peeled and deveined shrimp onto the soaked wooden skewers, about 4-5 shrimp per skewer.
3. Brush the shrimp skewers with the marinade, ensuring they are coated evenly.
4. Preheat your smoker to 225°F (110°C) using the wood chips you choose for smoke flavor.
5. Place the shrimp skewers on the smoker grate.

6. Smoke the shrimp for approximately 20-30 minutes or until they are opaque and have a smoky flavor.
7. Once done, remove the smoked paprika shrimp skewers from the smoker and serve them as an appetizer or a main dish. Enjoy!

Smoked Teriyaki Tofu

Smoked Teriyaki Tofu is a flavorful and vegetarian option for those who love the taste of smoked dishes. The tofu absorbs the smoky essence and teriyaki sauce beautifully, making it a satisfying and healthy choice.

Prep Time:15 minutes

Ingredients:

- ✓ 1 block of extra-firm tofu
- ✓ 1/2 cup teriyaki sauce
- ✓ 2 tablespoons soy sauce
- ✓ 2 cloves garlic, minced
- ✓ 1 teaspoon ginger, grated
- ✓ 1 tablespoon sesame oil
- ✓ Wood chips for smoking (e.g., cherry or oak)

Method:

1. Press the tofu to remove excess moisture. Slice the block into 1/2-inch thick slabs.
2. Mix the teriyaki sauce, soy sauce, minced garlic, grated ginger, and sesame oil in a bowl to create a marinade.
3. Place the tofu slabs in a shallow dish and pour the marinade over them. Allow the tofu to marinate for at least 30 minutes, flipping occasionally to ensure even coverage.
4. Preheat your smoker to 225°F (110°C) using the wood chips you choose for smoke flavor.
5. Place the marinated tofu slabs on the smoker grate.

6. Smoke the tofu for approximately 1-1.5 hours or until it has a slightly firm texture and absorbs a smoky flavor.
7. Once done, remove the smoked teriyaki tofu from the smoker and serve as a main dish with rice or noodles, or use it in wraps and salads. Enjoy your vegetarian smoked delight!

Pecan-Smoked Ribeye Steak

Pecan-smoked ribeye Steak is a luxurious treat for steak enthusiasts. The rich, nutty flavor of pecan wood smoke enhances the succulent ribeye, making it an unforgettable meal.

Prep Time:15 minutes

Ingredients:

- ✓ 2 ribeye steaks (1.5 inches thick)
- ✓ 2 tablespoons olive oil
- ✓ 2 teaspoons coarse salt
- ✓ 1 teaspoon black pepper
- ✓ 1 teaspoon garlic powder
- ✓ Pecan wood chunks or chips for smoking

Method:

1. Preheat your smoker to 225°F (110°C) using pecan wood chunks or chips for smoke flavor.
2. Brush both sides of the ribeye steaks with olive oil.
3. Mix the coarse salt, black pepper, and garlic powder in a small bowl to blend the seasoning.
4. Sprinkle the seasoning blend evenly over both sides of the steaks, patting it gently to adhere.
5. Place the seasoned ribeye steaks on the smoker grate.
6. Smoke the steaks for approximately 1-1.5 hours or until they reach your desired level of doneness (for medium-rare, aim for an internal temperature of 130-135°F or 54-57°C).

7. Once done, remove the pecan-smoked ribeye steaks from the smoker and let them rest for a few minutes before slicing and serving. Enjoy the smoky, savory goodness!

Cedar-Plank Smoked Trout

Cedar-Plank Smoked Trout is a delightful way to enjoy fresh fish with a smoky twist. The cedar plank imparts a wonderful aroma while keeping the trout moist and flavorful.

Prep Time:15 minutes

Ingredients:

- ✓ 2 whole trout, gutted and cleaned
- ✓ Cedar planks (soaked in water for 1-2 hours)
- ✓ 2 tablespoons olive oil
- ✓ 2 teaspoons lemon juice
- ✓ 1 teaspoon fresh dill, chopped
- ✓ 1 teaspoon fresh thyme, chopped
- ✓ Salt and black pepper to taste

Method:

1. Preheat your smoker to 225°F (110°C).
2. Mix the olive oil, lemon juice, chopped dill, chopped thyme, salt, and black pepper in a small bowl to create a marinade.
3. Pat the cleaned trout dry with paper towels, inside and out.
4. Brush the inside and outside of each trout with the marinade.
5. Place the soaked cedar planks on the smoker grate.
6. Lay the marinated trout on top of the cedar planks.
7. Smoke the trout for approximately 30-45 minutes or until they are cooked through and have a smoky flavor.

8. Carefully remove the cedar-plank smoked trout from the smoker and serve whole or filleted. Enjoy the unique flavor and aroma!

Smoked Vegetarian Chili

Smoked Vegetarian Chili is a hearty and flavorful dish that combines the smokiness of the grill with a medley of beans and vegetables. It's a comforting and satisfying meal.

Prep Time:15 minutes

Ingredients:

- ✓ 2 cans (15 ounces each) black beans, drained and rinsed
- ✓ 1 can (15 ounces) kidney beans, drained and rinsed
- ✓ 1 can (15 ounces) pinto beans, drained and rinsed
- ✓ 1 can (28 ounces) crushed tomatoes
- ✓ 1 onion, diced
- ✓ 2 bell peppers (any color), diced
- ✓ 2 cloves garlic, minced
- ✓ 2 tablespoons olive oil
- ✓ 2 teaspoons chili powder
- ✓ 1 teaspoon smoked paprika
- ✓ 1/2 teaspoon cayenne pepper (adjust for heat preference)
- ✓ Salt and black pepper to taste
- ✓ Wood chips for smoking (e.g., mesquite or hickory)

Method:

1. Preheat your smoker to 225°F (110°C) using the wood chips you choose for smoke flavor.
2. Heat the olive oil over medium heat on the smoker grate in a large cast-iron skillet or heatproof pan.

3. Add the diced onion, bell peppers, and minced garlic. Sauté until the vegetables are softened, about 5-7 minutes.
4. Stir in the chili powder, smoked paprika, cayenne, salt, and black pepper. Cook for an additional 2 minutes to toast the spices.
5. Add the drained and rinsed black beans, kidney beans, pinto beans, and crushed tomatoes to the skillet. Stir to combine.
6. Place the skillet in the smoker and smoke for 1-1.5 hours to infuse the chili with smoky flavor. Stir occasionally.
7. Remove the smoked vegetarian chili from the smoker and serve it hot. Garnish with your favorite toppings, such as shredded cheese, sour cream, or chopped green onions. Enjoy your smoky and satisfying chili!

Smoked Stuffed Bell Peppers

Smoked Stuffed Bell Peppers are a delicious and wholesome dish combining smoky flavors and hearty filling. These stuffed peppers make for a satisfying meal or a delightful side dish.

Prep Time:15 minutes

Ingredients:

- ✓ 4 large bell peppers (any color)
- ✓ 1 cup cooked rice
- ✓ 1 cup ground beef or turkey (cooked and seasoned)
- ✓ 1/2 cup black beans (canned and drained)
- ✓ 1/2 cup corn kernels (fresh, frozen, or canned)
- ✓ 1/2 cup diced tomatoes
- ✓ 1/2 cup shredded cheddar cheese
- ✓ 1/4 cup diced onion
- ✓ 2 cloves garlic, minced
- ✓ 2 teaspoons chili powder
- ✓ 1 teaspoon smoked paprika
- ✓ Salt and black pepper to taste
- ✓ Wood chips for smoking (e.g., oak or applewood)

Method:

1. Cut the tops off the bell peppers and remove the seeds and membranes to create hollow shells.
2. Combine the cooked rice, seasoned ground meat, black beans, corn kernels, diced tomatoes, shredded cheddar cheese, diced onion, minced garlic, chili powder, smoked

paprika, salt, and black pepper in a large bowl. Mix well to create the filling.

3. Stuff each bell pepper with the filling mixture, packing it down gently.
4. Preheat your smoker to 225°F (110°C) using the wood chips you choose for smoke flavor.
5. Place the stuffed bell peppers on the smoker grate.
6. Smoke the stuffed bell peppers for approximately 2-2.5 hours, or until the peppers are tender and the filling is heated through and has a smoky flavor.
7. Once done, remove the smoked stuffed bell peppers from the smoker and let them cool for a few minutes before serving. Enjoy your flavorful and smoky stuffed peppers!

Smoked Pineapple Salsa

Smoked Pineapple Salsa is a sweet, tangy, and smoky twist on traditional salsa. It pairs perfectly with grilled meats and tacos or as a flavorful dip for tortilla chips.

Prep Time:15 minutes

Ingredients:

- ✓ 1 ripe pineapple, peeled, cored, and sliced into rings
- ✓ 1 red onion, thinly sliced
- ✓ 2 jalapeño peppers, seeded and finely diced
- ✓ 1 red bell pepper, diced
- ✓ 1/4 cup fresh cilantro, chopped
- ✓ Juice of 2 limes
- ✓ 1 tablespoon olive oil
- ✓ Salt and black pepper to taste
- ✓ Wood chips for smoking (e.g., mesquite or cherry)

Method:

1. Preheat your smoker to 225°F (110°C) using the wood chips you choose for smoke flavor.
2. Place the pineapple rings on the smoker grate and smoke for about 30-45 minutes until they develop a smoky flavor and are slightly caramelized. Remove and let them cool.
3. Dice the smoked pineapple into small pieces.
4. Combine the diced smoked pineapple, thinly sliced red onion, finely diced jalapeño peppers, red bell pepper, and chopped fresh cilantro in a large bowl.

5. Drizzle the lime juice and olive oil over the mixture and toss to combine.
6. Season the smoked pineapple salsa with salt and black pepper to taste.
7. Refrigerate the salsa for at least 30 minutes before serving to allow the flavors to meld. Serve as a topping for grilled meats or a zesty dip for tortilla chips. Enjoy the sweet and smoky goodness!

Smoked Onion and Mushroom Soup

Smoked Onion and Mushroom Soup is a rich and hearty soup with a smoky twist. The depth of flavor from smoked onions and mushrooms makes this a comforting and satisfying dish.

Prep Time:15 minutes

Ingredients:

- ✓ 4 large onions, peeled and halved
- ✓ 2 cups mushrooms, sliced
- ✓ 4 cloves garlic, minced
- ✓ 4 cups vegetable broth
- ✓ 2 tablespoons olive oil
- ✓ 1 teaspoon thyme
- ✓ 1 teaspoon smoked paprika
- ✓ Salt and black pepper to taste
- ✓ Wood chips for smoking (e.g., oak or hickory)

Method:

1. Preheat your smoker to 225°F (110°C) using the wood chips you choose for smoke flavor.
2. Place the halved onions and sliced mushrooms on the smoker grate.
3. Smoke the onions and mushrooms for about 45 minutes to 1 hour or until they are tender and have a smoky flavor. Remove and set aside.
4. Heat the olive oil over medium heat in a large pot or Dutch oven.

5. Add the minced garlic and sauté for about 1-2 minutes until fragrant.
6. Stir in the smoked onions and mushrooms, and cook for 5 minutes.
7. Add the vegetable broth, thyme, smoked paprika, salt, and black pepper. Bring the mixture to a simmer.
8. Cover and simmer for 20-25 minutes, allowing the flavors to meld.
9. Blend the soup until smooth and creamy using an immersion or a regular blender.
10. Taste and adjust the seasoning if needed.
11. Serve hot smoked onion and mushroom soup, garnished with additional smoked mushrooms or fresh herbs if desired. Enjoy this smoky and comforting soup!

Smoked Gouda and Bacon Dip

Smoked Gouda and Bacon Dip is a creamy and savory appetizer for gatherings. The smoky Gouda and crispy bacon make it an irresistible crowd-pleaser.

Prep Time:15 minutes

Ingredients:

- ✓ 8 ounces cream cheese, softened
- ✓ 1 cup sour cream
- ✓ 1 cup smoked Gouda cheese, shredded
- ✓ 1/2 cup cooked bacon, crumbled
- ✓ 2 green onions, thinly sliced
- ✓ 1 teaspoon smoked paprika
- ✓ 1/2 teaspoon garlic powder
- ✓ Salt and black pepper to taste
- ✓ Wood chips for smoking (e.g., applewood or mesquite)

Method:

1. Preheat your smoker to 225°F (110°C) using the wood chips you choose for smoke flavor.
2. Combine the softened cream cheese, sour cream, shredded smoked Gouda cheese, crumbled bacon, thinly sliced green onions, smoked paprika, garlic powder, salt, and black pepper in a mixing bowl. Mix until well combined.
3. Transfer the mixture to a heatproof dish suitable for smoking.

4. Place the dish on the smoker grate and smoke for approximately 30-45 minutes, or until the dip has absorbed a smoky flavor and is heated through.
5. Once done, remove the smoked Gouda and bacon dip from the smoker and serve it hot with your favorite dippers, such as tortilla chips, crackers, or vegetable sticks. Enjoy the creamy and smoky goodness!

Smoked Artichoke Hearts

Smoked Artichoke Hearts are a unique and flavorful appetizer or side dish. The smoky twist adds depth to the tender artichoke hearts, making them a delightful addition to your meal.

Prep Time:15 minutes

Ingredients:

- ✓ 1 can (14 ounces) artichoke hearts, drained and halved
- ✓ 2 tablespoons olive oil
- ✓ 2 cloves garlic, minced
- ✓ 1 teaspoon lemon juice
- ✓ 1/2 teaspoon smoked paprika
- ✓ Salt and black pepper to taste
- ✓ Wood chips for smoking (e.g., cherry or pecan)

Method:

1. Preheat your smoker to 225°F (110°C) using the wood chips you choose for smoke flavor.
2. Mix the olive oil, minced garlic, lemon juice, smoked paprika, salt, and black pepper in a bowl to create a marinade.
3. Add the drained and halved artichoke hearts to the marinade, tossing to coat them evenly.
4. Place the marinated artichoke hearts on a grill pan or a heatproof dish suitable for smoking.
5. Put the grill pan or dish on the smoker grate.

6. Smoke the artichoke hearts for approximately 30-45 minutes or until they are tender and have absorbed a smoky flavor.

7. Once done, remove the smoked artichoke hearts from the smoker and serve them as a unique and flavorful appetizer or side dish. Enjoy!

Smoked Portobello Mushrooms

Smoked Portobello Mushrooms are a versatile and delicious dish that can be served as a side, a burger substitute, or a topping for salads and pizzas. The smoky flavor enhances the meaty texture of the Portobello mushrooms.

Prep Time:15 minutes

Ingredients:

- ✓ 4 large Portobello mushrooms, stems removed
- ✓ 2 tablespoons olive oil
- ✓ 2 cloves garlic, minced
- ✓ 1 teaspoon balsamic vinegar
- ✓ 1/2 teaspoon smoked paprika
- ✓ Salt and black pepper to taste
- ✓ Wood chips for smoking (e.g., oak or mesquite)

Method:

1. Preheat your smoker to 225°F (110°C) using the wood chips you choose for smoke flavor.
2. Mix the olive oil, minced garlic, balsamic vinegar, smoked paprika, salt, and black pepper in a bowl to create a marinade.
3. Brush both sides of the Portobello mushrooms with the marinade, ensuring they are coated evenly.
4. Place the mushrooms on the smoker grate, gill side down.

5. Smoke the Portobello mushrooms for approximately 45-60 minutes or until they are tender and have a smoky flavor.
6. Once done, remove the smoked Portobello mushrooms from the smoker and serve them as a side dish, burger substitute, or topping for salads and pizzas. Enjoy the rich, smoky goodness!

Smoked Cheddar and Beer Soup

Smoked Cheddar and Beer Soup is a hearty and flavorful comfort food that combines the smoky richness of cheddar cheese with the bold flavors of beer. It's the perfect soup for a cozy evening.

Prep Time:15 minutes

Ingredients:

- ✓ 4 tablespoons unsalted butter
- ✓ 1 onion, diced
- ✓ 2 cloves garlic, minced
- ✓ 1/4 cup all-purpose flour
- ✓ 2 cups chicken or vegetable broth
- ✓ 2 cups beer (choose your favorite)
- ✓ 2 cups milk
- ✓ 2 cups shredded smoked cheddar cheese
- ✓ 1 teaspoon smoked paprika
- ✓ Salt and black pepper to taste
- ✓ Chopped chives or scallions for garnish (optional)
- ✓ Wood chips for smoking (e.g., hickory or applewood)

Method:

1. Preheat your smoker to 225°F (110°C) using the wood chips you choose for smoke flavor.
2. Melt the unsalted butter over medium heat in a large pot or Dutch oven.

3. Add the diced onion and minced garlic to the pot and sauté for about 5 minutes or until the onion is translucent.
4. Sprinkle the all-purpose flour over the onions and garlic and stir well to create a roux. Cook for 2-3 minutes, stirring constantly to prevent burning.
5. Gradually add the chicken or vegetable broth, beer, and milk to the pot, stirring continuously to avoid lumps.
6. Bring the mixture to a simmer and cook for 10-15 minutes, allowing it to thicken.
7. Stir in the shredded smoked cheddar cheese and smoked paprika until the cheese is fully melted and the soup is smooth.
8. Season the smoked cheddar and beer soup with salt and black pepper to taste.
9. Place the pot on the smoker grate and smoke the soup for 15-20 minutes to infuse it with smoky flavor. Stir occasionally.
10. Remove the smoked cheddar and beer soup from the smoker and spoon it into bowls. Garnish with chopped chives or scallions if desired. Enjoy this smoky and comforting soup!

Smoked Sweet Potato Fries

Smoked Sweet Potato Fries are a delicious and healthier alternative to regular fries. The smoky flavor enhances the natural sweetness of the sweet potatoes, making them a delightful snack or side dish.

Prep Time:15 minutes

Ingredients:

- ✓ 2 large sweet potatoes, peeled and cut into fries
- ✓ 2 tablespoons olive oil
- ✓ 1 teaspoon smoked paprika
- ✓ 1/2 teaspoon garlic powder
- ✓ 1/2 teaspoon onion powder
- ✓ Salt and black pepper to taste
- ✓ Wood chips for smoking (e.g., maple or pecan)

Method:

1. Preheat your smoker to 225°F (110°C) using the wood chips you choose for smoke flavor.
2. Toss the sweet potato fries in a large bowl with olive oil, smoked paprika, garlic powder, onion powder, salt, and black pepper. Make sure the fries are evenly coated with the seasoning.
3. Place the seasoned sweet potato fries on a wire rack or a grill pan suitable for smoking.
4. Put the wire rack or grill pan on the smoker grate.

5. Smoke the sweet potato fries for approximately 45-60 minutes or until they are tender inside and have a smoky flavor. Turn them occasionally for even smoking.
6. Once done, remove the smoked sweet potato fries from the smoker and serve them hot as a snack or side dish. Enjoy the smoky-sweet goodness!

Smoked Garlic Hummus

Smoked Garlic Hummus is a flavorful twist on traditional hummus, with the added depth of smoky roasted garlic. It's perfect for dipping with pita bread, vegetables, or as a spread.

Prep Time:15 minutes

Ingredients:

- ✓ 2 cans (15 ounces each) chickpeas, drained and rinsed
- ✓ 1 head of garlic
- ✓ 1/4 cup tahini
- ✓ 1/4 cup lemon juice
- ✓ 3 tablespoons olive oil
- ✓ 1 teaspoon smoked paprika
- ✓ Salt and black pepper to taste
- ✓ Wood chips for smoking (e.g., mesquite or hickory)

Method:

1. Preheat your smoker to 225°F (110°C) using the wood chips you choose for smoke flavor.
2. Cut the top off the head of garlic to expose the cloves. Place the garlic head on a piece of aluminum foil, drizzle with a bit of olive oil, and wrap it tightly in the foil.
3. Place the wrapped garlic on the smoker grate and smoke for about 30-45 minutes, or until the garlic cloves are soft and have absorbed a smoky flavor. Remove and let cool.

4. In a food processor, combine the smoked chickpeas, tahini, lemon juice, smoked paprika, and roasted garlic cloves (squeeze the softened cloves out of their skins).
5. Pulse the mixture until it becomes a smooth and creamy hummus. If needed, add a bit of water to achieve your desired consistency.
6. Season the smoked garlic hummus with salt and black pepper to taste, and pulse once more to combine.
7. Transfer the hummus to a serving bowl, drizzle with olive oil, and sprinkle with a pinch of smoked paprika for garnish.
8. Serve the smoked garlic hummus with pita bread and fresh vegetables or as a sandwich. Enjoy the smoky and savory flavors!

Smoked Avocado Guacamole

Smoked Avocado Guacamole is a unique and flavorful take on the classic dip. The smoky twist adds depth to the creamy avocados and enhances the overall taste.

Prep Time:15 minutes

Ingredients:

- ✓ 3 ripe avocados, peeled and pitted
- ✓ 1/2 cup diced tomatoes
- ✓ 1/4 cup diced red onion
- ✓ 2 cloves garlic, minced
- ✓ 2 tablespoons fresh cilantro, chopped
- ✓ 1 jalapeño pepper, seeded and finely diced
- ✓ Juice of 2 limes
- ✓ 1 teaspoon smoked paprika
- ✓ Salt and black pepper to taste
- ✓ Wood chips for smoking (e.g., applewood or mesquite)

Method:

1. Preheat your smoker to 225°F (110°C) using the wood chips you choose for smoke flavor.
2. Cut the ripe avocados into chunks and place them in a bowl.
3. Place the bowl of avocados on the smoker grate and smoke for about 30-45 minutes or until they develop a smoky flavor. Remove and let cool.

4. Mix the diced tomatoes, red onion, minced garlic, chopped cilantro, finely diced jalapeño pepper, and smoked paprika in a separate bowl.
5. Add the smoked avocados to the bowl and mash them with a fork or potato masher until you achieve your desired level of creaminess.
6. Squeeze the juice of 2 limes into the mixture and stir to combine.
7. Season the smoked avocado guacamole with salt and black pepper to taste. Adjust the lime juice, salt, and pepper as needed.
8. Serve the guacamole with tortilla chips as a topping for tacos or alongside your favorite Mexican dishes. Enjoy the smoky and creamy delight!

Smoked Mango Salsa

Smoked Mango Salsa is a sweet and savory twist on traditional salsa with the added dimension of smoky flavors. It's a delightful condiment that pairs well with grilled meats and fish or as a topping for tacos and salads.

Prep Time:15 minutes

Ingredients:

- ✓ 2 ripe mangoes, peeled, pitted, and diced
- ✓ 1 red bell pepper, diced
- ✓ 1 red onion, finely diced
- ✓ 1 jalapeño pepper, seeded and finely diced
- ✓ Juice of 2 limes
- ✓ 1/4 cup fresh cilantro, chopped
- ✓ 1 teaspoon smoked paprika
- ✓ Salt and black pepper to taste
- ✓ Wood chips for smoking (e.g., cherry or pecan)

Method:

1. Preheat your smoker to 225°F (110°C) using the wood chips you choose for smoke flavor.
2. Combine the diced mangoes, red bell pepper, red onion, jalapeño pepper, and chopped cilantro in a large bowl.
3. Squeeze the juice of 2 limes over the mixture.
4. Sprinkle the smoked paprika over the ingredients and toss to combine.

5. Place the bowl of salsa on the smoker grate and smoke for about 30-45 minutes, or until the salsa has absorbed a smoky flavor. Stir occasionally.
6. Once done, remove the smoked mango salsa from the smoker and season it with salt and black pepper to taste.
7. Serve the salsa as a topping for grilled meats, fish, or tacos or as a vibrant accompaniment to your favorite dishes. Enjoy the sweet and smoky fusion of flavors!

Smoked Eggplant Baba Ganoush

Smoked Eggplant Baba Ganoush is a smoky, creamy dip favorite in Middle Eastern cuisine. The rich and earthy flavor of smoked eggplant combines with tahini and other ingredients to create a delightful appetizer or spread.

Prep Time:15 minutes

Ingredients:

- ✓ 2 large eggplants
- ✓ 1/4 cup tahini
- ✓ 2 cloves garlic, minced
- ✓ Juice of 1 lemon
- ✓ 2 tablespoons olive oil
- ✓ 1/2 teaspoon smoked paprika
- ✓ Salt and black pepper to taste
- ✓ Fresh parsley for garnish (optional)
- ✓ Wood chips for smoking (e.g., mesquite or hickory)

Method:

1. Preheat your smoker to 225°F (110°C) using the wood chips you choose for smoke flavor.
2. Pierce the eggplants several times with a fork to allow for even smoking.
3. Place the eggplants directly on the smoker grate.
4. Smoke the eggplants for approximately 45-60 minutes, turning them occasionally until the skin is charred and the flesh is tender and smoky.

5. Remove the smoked eggplants from the smoker and let them cool slightly.
6. Once cooled, peel the skin off the eggplants and discard it.
7. Combine the smoked eggplant flesh, tahini, minced garlic, lemon juice, olive oil, smoked paprika, salt, and black pepper in a food processor.
8. Process the mixture until it becomes smooth and creamy. If needed, adjust the seasoning or add more lemon juice.
9. Transfer the smoked eggplant baba ganoush to a serving dish.
10.Garnish with fresh parsley and drizzle with olive oil.
11.Serve the baba ganoush as a dip with pita bread, crackers, or fresh vegetables. Enjoy the smoky and creamy dip!

Smoked Corn on the Cob

Smoked Corn on the Cob is a delightful, smoky side dish perfect for outdoor gatherings. The corn is infused with a smoky flavor, making it a favorite during summer cookouts.

Prep Time:15 minutes

Ingredients:

✓ 4 ears of fresh corn on the cob, husked and cleaned
✓ 2 tablespoons butter, melted
✓ Salt and black pepper to taste
✓ Wood chips for smoking (e.g., applewood or hickory)

Method:

1. Preheat your smoker to 225°F (110°C) using the wood chips you choose for smoke flavor.
2. Brush each ear of corn with melted butter, ensuring they are evenly coated.
3. Season the corn with salt and black pepper to taste.
4. Place the corn on the smoker grate.
5. Smoke the corn for approximately 45-60 minutes or until it is tender and has a smoky flavor. Turn the corn occasionally for even smoking.
6. Once done, remove the smoked corn on the cob from the smoker and serve it hot. Enjoy the smoky and savory goodness!

Smoked Cabbage Steaks

Smoked Cabbage Steaks are a unique and flavorful side dish. The smoky flavor enhances the natural sweetness of cabbage, creating a delicious and healthy accompaniment to your meal.

Prep Time:15 minutes

Ingredients:

- ✓ 1 head of green cabbage
- ✓ 2 tablespoons olive oil
- ✓ 1 teaspoon smoked paprika
- ✓ 1/2 teaspoon garlic powder
- ✓ Salt and black pepper to taste
- ✓ Wood chips for smoking (e.g., oak or mesquite)

Method:

1. Preheat your smoker to 225°F (110°C) using the wood chips you choose for smoke flavor.
2. Cut the head of cabbage into 1-inch thick slices, creating "cabbage steaks."
3. Combine the olive oil, smoked paprika, garlic powder, salt, and black pepper in a small bowl to create a seasoning blend.
4. Brush both sides of each cabbage steak with the seasoning blend, ensuring they are coated evenly.
5. Place the seasoned cabbage steaks on a grill pan or a wire rack suitable for smoking.
6. Put the grill pan or wire rack on the smoker grate.

7. Smoke the cabbage steaks for approximately 45-60 minutes or until they are tender and have a smoky flavor. Turn them occasionally for even smoking.

8. Once done, remove the smoked cabbage steaks from the smoker and serve them hot. Enjoy the smoky and savory cabbage steaks!

Smoked Brussels Sprouts with Bacon

Smoked Brussels Sprouts with Bacon is a delightful side dish that combines the smokiness of bacon with the earthy flavors of Brussels sprouts. It's a perfect accompaniment to your main course.

Prep Time:15 minutes

Ingredients:

- ✓ 1 pound Brussels sprouts, trimmed and halved
- ✓ 4 slices bacon, diced
- ✓ 2 tablespoons olive oil
- ✓ 2 cloves garlic, minced
- ✓ 1/2 teaspoon smoked paprika
- ✓ Salt and black pepper to taste
- ✓ Wood chips for smoking (e.g., cherry or hickory)

Method:

1. Preheat your smoker to 225°F (110°C) using the wood chips you choose for smoke flavor.
2. Toss the halved Brussels sprouts in a large bowl with olive oil, minced garlic, smoked paprika, salt, and black pepper. Make sure the Brussels sprouts are evenly coated.
3. Place the diced bacon in a cast-iron skillet or heatproof pan suitable for smoking.
4. Put the skillet or pan on the smoker grate.

5. Smoke the bacon for about 30 minutes or until it becomes crispy and has absorbed a smoky flavor. Remove and set aside.
6. Add seasoned Brussels sprouts in the same skillet or pan.
7. Smoke the Brussels sprouts for approximately 45-60 minutes or until they are tender and have a smoky flavor. Stir occasionally.
8. Once done, remove the smoked Brussels sprouts from the smoker and toss them with the crispy smoked bacon.
9. Serve the smoked Brussels sprouts with bacon as a flavorful side dish. Enjoy the smoky and savory combination!

Smoked Asparagus Bundles

Smoked Asparagus Bundles are an elegant, flavorful side dish perfect for special occasions. The smoky essence enhances the natural sweetness of asparagus, creating a delightful and visually appealing dish.

Prep Time:15 minutes

Ingredients:

- ✓ 1 bunch of asparagus spears, tough ends trimmed
- ✓ 4 slices prosciutto or bacon
- ✓ 2 tablespoons olive oil
- ✓ 1 teaspoon lemon zest
- ✓ 1/2 teaspoon smoked paprika
- ✓ Salt and black pepper to taste
- ✓ Wood chips for smoking (e.g., applewood or pecan)

Method:

1. Preheat your smoker to 225°F (110°C) using the wood chips you choose for smoke flavor.
2. Divide the asparagus spears into equal-sized bundles, typically 3-4 spears per bundle.
3. Wrap each bundle with a slice of prosciutto or bacon, securing it in place.
4. In a small bowl, combine the olive oil, lemon zest, smoked paprika, salt, and black pepper to create a seasoning blend.
5. Brush the seasoned oil mixture over the asparagus bundles, ensuring they are coated evenly.

6. Place the asparagus bundles on a wire rack suitable for smoking.
7. Put the wire rack on the smoker grate.
8. Smoke the asparagus bundles for approximately 30-45 minutes or until the asparagus is tender and has a smoky flavor.
9. Once done, remove the smoked asparagus bundles from the smoker and serve them hot. Enjoy this elegant and smoky side dish!

Smoked Tomato and Basil Salad

Smoked Tomato and Basil Salad is a refreshing and smoky twist on a classic Caprese salad. Combining smoky tomatoes, fresh basil, and creamy mozzarella is a delightful appetizer.

Prep Time:15 minutes

Ingredients:

- ✓ 4 large tomatoes, sliced
- ✓ 8 ounces fresh mozzarella cheese, sliced
- ✓ 1/2 cup fresh basil leaves
- ✓ 2 tablespoons olive oil
- ✓ Balsamic glaze for drizzling
- ✓ Salt and black pepper to taste
- ✓ Wood chips for smoking (e.g., cherry or oak)

Method:

1. Preheat your smoker to 225°F (110°C) using the wood chips you choose for smoke flavor.
2. Place the tomato slices on the smoker grate.
3. Smoke the tomato slices for 30-45 minutes or until they are slightly softened and have a smoky flavor.
4. Remove the smoked tomato slices from the smoker and let them cool slightly.
5. On a serving platter, arrange the smoked tomato slices, fresh mozzarella slices, and fresh basil leaves in an alternating pattern.
6. Drizzle olive oil over the salad and season with salt and black pepper to taste.

7. Finish the smoked tomato and basil salad with a drizzle of balsamic glaze for added sweetness and depth of flavor.

8. Serve the salad as an appetizer or side dish. Enjoy the smoky and refreshing combination!

Smoked Caprese Skewers

Smoked Caprese Skewers are a delightful and portable twist on the classic Caprese salad. The smoky flavors complement the fresh ingredients, making these skewers a perfect appetizer or party snack.

Prep Time:15 minutes

Ingredients:

- ✓ Cherry tomatoes
- ✓ Fresh mozzarella balls (bocconcini)
- ✓ Fresh basil leaves
- ✓ Balsamic glaze for drizzling
- ✓ Wooden skewers soaked in water
- ✓ Wood chips for smoking (e.g., applewood or mesquite)

Method:

1. Preheat your smoker to 225°F (110°C) using the wood chips you choose for smoke flavor.
2. Thread a cherry tomato, a mozzarella ball, and a fresh basil leaf onto each wooden skewer, repeating as desired to create multiple skewers.
3. Place the skewers on the smoker grate.
4. Smoke the Caprese skewers for 15-20 minutes or until the tomatoes are slightly softened and have a smoky flavor.
5. Remove the smoked Caprese skewers from the smoker and let them cool slightly.

6. Drizzle balsamic glaze over the skewers for added sweetness and depth of flavor.
7. Serve the smoked Caprese skewers as a delightful appetizer or party snack. Enjoy the smoky and portable goodness!

Smoked Watermelon Salad

Smoked Watermelon Salad is a unique and refreshing dish that combines the natural sweetness of watermelon with a hint of smokiness. It's a perfect side dish for summer gatherings.

Prep Time:15 minutes

Ingredients:

- ✓ 1 small seedless watermelon cut into cubes
- ✓ 1/4 cup fresh mint leaves, chopped
- ✓ 1/4 cup crumbled feta cheese
- ✓ Juice of 1 lime
- ✓ 1 tablespoon honey
- ✓ Salt and black pepper to taste
- ✓ Wood chips for smoking (e.g., applewood or cherry)

Method:

1. Preheat your smoker to 225°F (110°C) using the wood chips you choose for smoke flavor.
2. Place the watermelon cubes on a wire rack or a grill pan suitable for smoking.
3. Put the wire rack or grill pan on the smoker grate.
4. Smoke the watermelon cubes for 15-20 minutes or until they develop a light smoky flavor. Be careful not to over-smoke; you want a subtle smokiness.
5. Remove the smoked watermelon cubes from the smoker and let them cool slightly.
6. Combine the smoked watermelon cubes, chopped fresh mint leaves, and crumbled feta cheese in a bowl.

7. Whisk the lime juice and honey in a separate small bowl to create a dressing.
8. Drizzle the lime and honey dressing over the salad and gently toss to combine.
9. Season the smoked watermelon salad with salt and black pepper to taste.
10. Serve the salad as a refreshing side dish for summer gatherings. Enjoy the sweet and smoky flavors!

Smoked Peach Cobbler

Smoked Peach Cobbler is a delicious and comforting dessert that combines the sweetness of peaches with a hint of smokiness. It's perfect for ending a barbecue feast with a touch of homey goodness.

Prep Time:15 minutes

Ingredients:

- ✓ 4 cups fresh or canned peaches, sliced
- ✓ 1 cup all-purpose flour
- ✓ 1 cup granulated sugar
- ✓ 1 cup milk
- ✓ 1/2 cup unsalted butter, melted
- ✓ 1 teaspoon vanilla extract
- ✓ 1/2 teaspoon ground cinnamon
- ✓ 1/4 teaspoon salt
- ✓ Wood chips for smoking (e.g., oak or hickory)

Method:

1. Preheat your smoker to 225°F (110°C) using the wood chips you choose for smoke flavor.
2. Place the sliced peaches in a heatproof dish suitable for smoking.
3. Put the dish on the smoker grate.
4. Smoke the peaches for about 30-45 minutes or until they are tender and have absorbed a smoky flavor. Remove and set aside.

5. Combine the all-purpose flour, granulated sugar, milk, melted unsalted butter, vanilla extract, ground cinnamon, and salt in a mixing bowl. Mix until smooth.
6. Pour the batter over the smoked peaches in the heatproof dish.
7. Place the dish back on the smoker grate.
8. Smoke the peach cobbler for approximately 45-60 minutes, or until the top is golden brown and the cobbler is bubbling.
9. Remove the smoked peach cobbler from the smoker and let it cool slightly.
10. Serve the cobbler warm, either on its own or with a scoop of vanilla ice cream for added indulgence. Enjoy the smoky and comforting dessert!

Smoked Blueberry Pie

Smoked Blueberry Pie is a delightful and fruity dessert with a smoky twist. Combining sweet blueberries and smoky flavors makes this pie a memorable treat.

Prep Time:15 minutes

Ingredients:

- ✓ 2 refrigerated pie crusts (or homemade if preferred)
- ✓ 4 cups fresh blueberries
- ✓ 1 cup granulated sugar
- ✓ 3 tablespoons cornstarch
- ✓ Juice of 1 lemon
- ✓ 1/2 teaspoon ground cinnamon
- ✓ 1/4 teaspoon salt
- ✓ Wood chips for smoking (e.g., hickory or cherry)

Method:

1. Preheat your smoker to 225°F (110°C) using the wood chips you choose for smoke flavor.
2. Place one of the pie crusts in a dish, pressing it firmly against the bottom and sides.
3. Combine the fresh blueberries, granulated sugar, cornstarch, lemon juice, ground cinnamon, and salt in a large mixing bowl. Mix until the blueberries are coated evenly.
4. Pour the blueberry mixture into the pie crust in the dish.
5. Place the second pie crust on top and crimp the edges to seal the pie.

6. Cut a few slits in the top crust to allow steam to escape.
7. Place the pie dish on the smoker grate.
8. Smoke the blueberry pie for approximately 60-75 minutes until the crust is golden brown and the blueberry filling is bubbling.
9. Remove the smoked blueberry pie from the smoker and let it cool.
10. Slice and serve the pie as a delicious dessert. Enjoy the sweet and smoky flavors!

Smoked Chocolate Brownies

Smoked Chocolate Brownies are a decadent, rich dessert with a delightful smoky twist. Combining dark chocolate and smokiness creates a unique and indulgent treat for chocolate lovers.

Prep Time:15 minutes

Ingredients:

- ✓ 1 cup (2 sticks) unsalted butter
- ✓ 2 cups granulated sugar
- ✓ 4 large eggs
- ✓ 1 teaspoon vanilla extract
- ✓ 1 cup all-purpose flour
- ✓ 1/2 cup unsweetened cocoa powder
- ✓ 1/2 teaspoon salt
- ✓ 1 cup dark chocolate chips
- ✓ Wood chips for smoking (e.g., oak or hickory)

Method:

1. Preheat your smoker to 225°F (110°C) using the wood chips you choose for smoke flavor.
2. In a saucepan, melt the unsalted butter over low heat. Once melted, remove it from the heat and let it cool slightly.
3. Whisk the granulated sugar, eggs, and vanilla extract in a mixing bowl until well combined.
4. Add melted butter to the sugar and egg mixture, whisking continuously.

5. Sift together the all-purpose flour, unsweetened cocoa powder, and salt in a separate bowl.
6. Gradually add the dry ingredients to the wet ingredients, stirring until the batter is smooth and well-mixed.
7. Fold in the dark chocolate chips.
8. Line a baking pan with parchment paper or aluminum foil, leaving some overhang for easy removal.
9. Pour the brownie batter into the prepared pan, spreading it evenly.
10. Place the baking pan on the smoker grate.
11. Smoke the brownies for approximately 60-75 minutes, or until a toothpick inserted into the center comes out with a few moist crumbs (avoid overbaking for fudgy brownies).
12. Remove the smoked chocolate brownies from the smoker and let them cool completely in the pan.
13. Lift the brownies out of the pan using the parchment paper or foil overhang, then cut them into squares.
14. Serve the smoked chocolate brownies as a decadent dessert. Enjoy the smoky and chocolaty goodness!

Smoked Pecan Pie

Smoked Pecan Pie is a classic Southern dessert with a smoky twist. The rich and nutty flavors of pecans are elevated with a hint of smokiness, making it a perfect treat for special occasions.

Prep Time:15 minutes

Ingredients:

- ✓ 1 refrigerated pie crust (or homemade if preferred)
- ✓ 1 1/2 cups pecan halves
- ✓ 3 large eggs
- ✓ 1 cup dark corn syrup
- ✓ 1/2 cup granulated sugar
- ✓ 2 tablespoons unsalted butter, melted
- ✓ 1 teaspoon vanilla extract
- ✓ 1/4 teaspoon salt
- ✓ Wood chips for smoking (e.g., pecan or hickory)

Method:

1. Preheat your smoker to 225°F (110°C) using the wood chips you choose for smoke flavor.
2. Place the pecan halves on a baking sheet and toast them in the smoker for 15-20 minutes or until they are lightly toasted and have a smoky aroma. Remove and set aside.
3. Line a pie dish with the refrigerated pie crust, pressing it firmly against the bottom and sides.

4. In a mixing bowl, whisk the eggs, dark corn syrup, granulated sugar, melted unsalted butter, vanilla extract, and salt until well combined.
5. Spread the toasted pecan halves evenly over the pie crust in the dish.
6. Pour the filling mixture over the pecans.
7. Place the pie dish on the smoker grate.
8. Smoke the pecan pie for approximately 60-75 minutes or until the filling is set and the top is golden brown.
9. Remove the smoked pecan pie from the smoker and let it cool completely.
10. Slice and serve the pie as a classic Southern dessert with a smoky twist. Enjoy the nutty and smoky flavors!

Smoked Pineapple Upside-Down Cake

Smoked Pineapple Upside-Down Cake is a tropical and smoky dessert for summer gatherings. The combination of sweet pineapple and smokiness makes it a delightful treat.

Prep Time:15 minutes

Ingredients:

- ✓ 1 can (20 ounces) pineapple slices in juice, drained (reserve the juice)
- ✓ 1/4 cup unsalted butter
- ✓ 3/4 cup brown sugar, packed
- ✓ Maraschino cherries (optional for garnish)
- ✓ 1 1/2 cups all-purpose flour
- ✓ 1 cup granulated sugar
- ✓ 1/3 cup unsalted butter, softened
- ✓ 1 1/2 teaspoons baking powder
- ✓ 1/2 teaspoon salt
- ✓ 1/2 cup reserved pineapple juice
- ✓ 2 large eggs
- ✓ 1 teaspoon vanilla extract
- ✓ Wood chips for smoking (e.g., cherry or applewood)

Method:

1. Preheat your smoker to 225°F (110°C) using the wood chips you choose for smoke flavor.
2. In a heatproof skillet or cake pan, melt the 1/4 cup unsalted butter over low heat on the stove. Once melted, remove from heat.

3. Sprinkle the brown sugar evenly over the melted butter in the skillet or pan.
4. Arrange the drained pineapple slices over the brown sugar in a decorative pattern. If desired, you can also place a maraschino cherry in the center of each pineapple slice.
5. Combine the all-purpose flour, granulated sugar, softened unsalted butter, baking powder, and salt in a mixing bowl. Mix until it resembles coarse crumbs.
6. Add the reserved pineapple juice, eggs, and vanilla extract to the dry mixture. Beat until the batter is smooth and well combined.
7. Pour the cake batter over the pineapple slices in the skillet or pan, spreading it evenly.
8. Place the skillet or pan on the smoker grate.
9. Smoke the pineapple upside-down cake for approximately 60-75 minutes, or until a toothpick inserted into the center comes out clean, and the top is golden brown.
10. Remove the smoked pineapple upside-down cake from the smoker and let it cool slightly.
11. Invert the cake onto a serving platter, making the pineapple slices the top.
12. Serve the cake warm or at room temperature as a tropical and smoky dessert. Enjoy the sweet and smoky flavors!

Smoked Banana Bread

Smoked Banana Bread is a moist and flavorful dessert with a subtle smoky twist. Ripe bananas and a hint of smokiness create a delightful treat for banana bread enthusiasts.

Prep Time:15 minutes

Ingredients:

- ✓ 3 ripe bananas, mashed
- ✓ 1/2 cup unsalted butter, melted
- ✓ 1 cup granulated sugar
- ✓ 2 large eggs
- ✓ 1 teaspoon vanilla extract
- ✓ 1 1/2 cups all-purpose flour
- ✓ 1 teaspoon baking soda
- ✓ 1/2 teaspoon salt
- ✓ 1/2 teaspoon ground cinnamon
- ✓ Wood chips for smoking (e.g., pecan or applewood)

Method:

1. Preheat your smoker to 225°F (110°C) using the wood chips you choose for smoke flavor.
2. Combine the mashed ripe bananas, melted unsalted butter, granulated sugar, eggs, and vanilla extract in a mixing bowl. Mix until well combined.
3. Whisk together the all-purpose flour, baking soda, salt, and ground cinnamon in a separate bowl.
4. Gradually add the dry ingredients to the banana mixture, stirring until the batter is smooth.

5. Line or grease a loaf pan with parchment paper to prevent sticking.
6. Pour the banana bread batter into the prepared loaf pan, spreading it evenly.
7. Place the loaf pan on the smoker grate.
8. Smoke the banana bread for approximately 60-75 minutes, or until a toothpick inserted into the center comes out clean and the top is golden brown.
9. Once done, remove the smoked banana bread from the smoker and let it cool in the pan for a few minutes.
10. Transfer the banana bread to a wire rack to cool completely.
11. Slice and serve the smoked banana bread as a moist and smoky dessert. Enjoy the banana and smoky goodness!

Smoked Apple Crisp

Smoked Apple Crisp is a comforting and smoky dessert that combines the sweetness of apples with a crispy topping. It's a perfect treat for cooler evenings and gatherings.

Prep Time:15 minutes

Ingredients:

- ✓ 4 cups apples, peeled, cored, and sliced (e.g., Granny Smith or Honeycrisp)
- ✓ 1 tablespoon lemon juice
- ✓ 1/2 cup granulated sugar
- ✓ 1 teaspoon ground cinnamon
- ✓ 1/4 teaspoon ground nutmeg
- ✓ 1/4 teaspoon salt
- ✓ 1 cup old-fashioned rolled oats
- ✓ 1/2 cup all-purpose flour
- ✓ 1/2 cup brown sugar, packed
- ✓ 1/2 cup unsalted butter, softened
- ✓ Wood chips for smoking (e.g., applewood or cherry)

Method:

1. Preheat your smoker to 225°F (110°C) using the wood chips you choose for smoke flavor.
2. In a mixing bowl, combine the sliced apples and lemon juice, tossing to coat the apples evenly.
3. Mix the granulated sugar, ground cinnamon, ground nutmeg, and salt in another bowl.

4. Sprinkle the sugar and spice mixture over the sliced apples and gently toss to coat the apples.
5. Combine the old-fashioned rolled oats, all-purpose flour, brown sugar, and softened unsalted butter in a separate bowl. Mix until the mixture resembles coarse crumbs.
6. Place the seasoned apple slices in a baking dish.
7. Sprinkle the oat and flour mixture evenly over the apples, covering them completely.
8. Place the baking dish on the smoker grate.
9. Smoke the apple crisp for approximately 60-75 minutes, or until the apples are tender, the filling is bubbly, and the topping is golden brown.
10. Remove the smoked apple crisp from the smoker and let it cool slightly.
11. Serve the apple crisp warm on its own or with a scoop of vanilla ice cream for added indulgence. Enjoy the sweet and smoky dessert!

Smoked Cherry Cobbler

Smoked Cherry Cobbler is a delightful and fruity dessert with a smoky twist. The combination of sweet cherries and a buttery cobbler topping, all infused with smokiness, makes it a perfect treat for any occasion.

Prep Time:15 minutes

Ingredients:

- ✓ 4 cups fresh or frozen cherries, pitted
- ✓ 1 cup granulated sugar
- ✓ 1/2 cup unsalted butter, melted
- ✓ 1 cup all-purpose flour
- ✓ 2 teaspoons baking powder
- ✓ 1/2 teaspoon salt
- ✓ 1 cup milk
- ✓ 1 teaspoon vanilla extract
- ✓ Wood chips for smoking (e.g., cherry or pecan)

Method:

1. Preheat your smoker to 225°F (110°C) using the wood chips you choose for smoke flavor.
2. Combine the pitted cherries and 1/2 cup of granulated sugar in a mixing bowl. Mix well and set aside to macerate for about 10 minutes.
3. Whisk together the all-purpose flour, remaining 1/2 cup of granulated sugar, baking powder, and salt in another bowl.

4. Add the melted unsalted butter, milk, and vanilla extract to the dry ingredients and stir until the batter is smooth.
5. Place the cherries in a baking dish.
6. Pour the batter evenly over the cherries in the baking dish.
7. Place the baking dish on the smoker grate.
8. Smoke the cherry cobbler for approximately 60-75 minutes or until the cobbler topping is golden brown and the filling is bubbling.
9. Remove the smoked cherry cobbler from the smoker and let it cool slightly.
10. Serve the cobbler warm, either on its own or with a scoop of vanilla ice cream for added indulgence. Enjoy the sweet and smoky dessert!

Smoked Almond Butter Cookies

Smoked Almond Butter Cookies are a nutty and smoky twist on classic butter cookies. Combining almond butter and a hint of smokiness creates a unique and delicious treat.

Prep Time:15 minutes

Ingredients:

- ✓ 1/2 cup unsalted butter, softened
- ✓ 1/2 cup almond butter
- ✓ 1/2 cup granulated sugar
- ✓ 1/2 cup brown sugar, packed
- ✓ 1 large egg
- ✓ 1 teaspoon vanilla extract
- ✓ 1 1/2 cups all-purpose flour
- ✓ 1/2 teaspoon baking soda
- ✓ 1/4 teaspoon salt
- ✓ Wood chips for smoking (e.g., pecan or hickory)

Method:

1. Preheat your smoker to 225°F (110°C) using the wood chips you choose for smoke flavor.
2. In a mixing bowl, cream the softened unsalted butter, almond butter, granulated sugar, and brown sugar until the mixture is light and fluffy.
3. Add the large egg and vanilla extract to the creamed mixture and beat until well combined.
4. Whisk together the all-purpose flour, baking soda, and salt in a separate bowl.

5. Gradually add the dry and wet ingredients, stirring until the cookie dough forms.
6. Drop spoonfuls of cookie dough onto a baking sheet lined with parchment paper.
7. Place the baking sheet on the smoker grate.
8. Smoke the almond butter cookies for approximately 30-40 minutes or until the cookies are lightly golden and have a subtle smoky flavor.
9. Remove the smoked almond butter cookies from the smoker and let them cool on the baking sheet.
10. Serve the cookies as a nutty and smoky treat. Enjoy the unique combination of almond butter and smokiness!

Smoked Coconut Macaroons

Smoked Coconut Macaroons are a sweet, smoky dessert perfect for coconut lovers. The combination of toasted coconut and smokiness creates a delightful treat.

Prep Time:15 minutes

Ingredients:

- ✓ 3 cups sweetened shredded coconut
- ✓ 2/3 cup granulated sugar
- ✓ 2 large egg whites
- ✓ 1/4 teaspoon salt
- ✓ 1/2 teaspoon vanilla extract
- ✓ Wood chips for smoking (e.g., applewood or cherry)

Method:

1. Preheat your smoker to 225°F (110°C) using the wood chips you choose for smoke flavor.
2. Spread the sweetened shredded coconut in a single layer on a baking sheet.
3. Place the baking sheet on the smoker grate.
4. Smoke the coconut for 15-20 minutes or until it becomes lightly toasted and has a smoky aroma. Stir occasionally for even toasting.
5. Whisk the granulated sugar, egg whites, salt, and vanilla extract in a mixing bowl until the mixture is well combined.
6. Add the smoked toasted coconut to the egg white mixture and gently fold until the coconut is coated.

7. Drop spoonfuls of the coconut mixture onto a baking sheet lined with parchment paper, forming mounds.
8. Place the baking sheet on the smoker grate.
9. Smoke the coconut macaroons for approximately 30-40 minutes or until they are lightly golden and have a subtle smoky flavor.
10. Remove the smoked coconut macaroons from the smoker and let them cool on the baking sheet.
11. Serve the macaroons as a sweet and smoky dessert. Enjoy the toasted coconut and smoky goodness!

Smoked Lemon Pound Cake

Smoked Lemon Pound Cake is a zesty and smoky dessert with lemon flavor. The combination of lemon zest and smokiness creates a delightful treat.

Prep Time:15 minutes

Ingredients:

- ✓ 1 cup unsalted butter, softened
- ✓ 2 cups granulated sugar
- ✓ 4 large eggs
- ✓ 2 teaspoons lemon zest
- ✓ 1 tablespoon lemon juice
- ✓ 1 teaspoon vanilla extract
- ✓ 2 cups all-purpose flour
- ✓ 1/2 teaspoon baking powder
- ✓ 1/2 teaspoon salt
- ✓ Powdered sugar for dusting (optional)
- ✓ Wood chips for smoking (e.g., lemon or cherry)

Method:

1. Preheat your smoker to 225°F (110°C) using the wood chips you choose for smoke flavor.
2. In a mixing bowl, cream the softened unsalted butter and granulated sugar until the mixture is light and fluffy.
3. Add the large eggs, one at a time, beating well after each addition.
4. Stir in the lemon zest, juice, and vanilla extract until well combined.

5. Whisk together the all-purpose flour, baking powder, and salt in a separate bowl.
6. Gradually add the dry ingredients to the wet ingredients, stirring until the cake batter is smooth.
7. Grease and flour a bundt pan or cake pan.
8. Pour the cake batter into the prepared pan, spreading it evenly.
9. Place the pan on the smoker grate.
10. Smoke the lemon pound cake for approximately 60-75 minutes, or until a toothpick inserted into the center comes out clean, and the top is golden brown.
11. Once done, remove the smoked lemon pound cake from the smoker and let it cool in the pan for a few minutes.
12. Invert the cake onto a serving platter.
13. Dust the top of the cake with powdered sugar if desired.
14. Slice and serve the pound cake as a zesty and smoky dessert. Enjoy the lemony and smoky flavors!

Smoked Pistachio Biscotti

Smoked Pistachio Biscotti are crunchy and nutty cookies with a delightful smoky twist. The combination of pistachios and smokiness creates a unique and satisfying treat.

Prep Time:15 minutes

Ingredients:

- ✓ 2 cups all-purpose flour
- ✓ 1 1/2 teaspoons baking powder
- ✓ 1/4 teaspoon salt
- ✓ 1/2 cup unsalted butter, softened
- ✓ 1 cup granulated sugar
- ✓ 2 large eggs
- ✓ 1 teaspoon vanilla extract
- ✓ 1 cup shelled pistachios, chopped
- ✓ Wood chips for smoking (e.g., pecan or hickory)

Method:

1. Preheat your smoker to 225°F (110°C) using the wood chips you choose for smoke flavor.
2. Whisk together the all-purpose flour, baking powder, and salt in a mixing bowl.
3. In another bowl, cream the softened unsalted butter and granulated sugar until the mixture is light and fluffy.
4. Add the large eggs and vanilla extract to the creamed mixture and beat until well combined.
5. Gradually add the dry ingredients to the wet ingredients, stirring until the biscotti dough forms.

6. Fold in the chopped pistachios.
7. Divide the dough and shape each half into a log on a baking sheet lined with parchment paper.
8. Place the baking sheet on the smoker grate.
9. Smoke the pistachio biscotti logs for approximately 30-40 minutes or until they are lightly golden and have a subtle smoky flavor. Rotate the logs halfway through for even smoking.
10. Once done, remove the smoked biscotti logs from the smoker and let them cool slightly on the baking sheet.
11. Using a sharp knife, slice the logs into individual biscotti cookies.
12. Return the sliced biscotti cookies to the baking sheet and bake in a preheated oven at 350°F (175°C) for 10-15 minutes or until crisp and golden.
13. Let the smoked pistachio biscotti cool completely before serving. Enjoy the crunchy and smoky cookies!

Smoked Cranberry Orange Muffins

Smoked Cranberry Orange Muffins are a delightful combination of tart cranberries and zesty orange with a subtle smoky twist. These muffins are perfect for breakfast or snacks, offering fruity and smoky flavors.

Prep Time:15 minutes

Ingredients:

- ✓ 2 cups all-purpose flour
- ✓ 1/2 cup granulated sugar
- ✓ 1 tablespoon baking powder
- ✓ 1/2 teaspoon salt
- ✓ 1/2 cup unsalted butter, melted and cooled
- ✓ 2 large eggs
- ✓ 1 cup whole milk
- ✓ Zest of 1 orange
- ✓ 1 cup fresh cranberries
- ✓ Wood chips for smoking (e.g., applewood or cherry)

Method:

1. Preheat your smoker to 225°F (110°C) using the wood chips you choose for smoke flavor.
2. Whisk together the all-purpose flour, granulated sugar, baking powder, and salt in a mixing bowl.
3. Whisk the melted and cooled unsalted butter, large eggs, whole milk, and orange zest in another bowl until well combined.

4. Gradually add the wet ingredients to the dry ingredients, stirring until the muffin batter is smooth.
5. Gently fold in the fresh cranberries.
6. Line or grease a muffin tin with paper liners to prevent sticking.
7. Fill each muffin cup about two-thirds full with the muffin batter.
8. Place the muffin tin on the smoker grate.
9. Smoke the cranberry orange muffins for approximately 30-40 minutes or until they are lightly golden, have risen, and have a subtle smoky flavor.
10. Once done, remove the smoked muffins from the smoker and let them cool in the tin for a few minutes.
11. Transfer the muffins to a wire rack to cool completely.
12. Serve the smoked cranberry orange muffins as a flavorful and smoky breakfast or snack. Enjoy the cranberry and orange goodness!

Smoked Vanilla Bean Ice Cream

Smoked Vanilla Bean Ice Cream is a creamy and smoky dessert that's perfect for ice cream enthusiasts. The combination of vanilla bean and smokiness creates a unique and delightful treat.

Prep Time:20 minutes

Ingredients:

- ✓ 2 cups heavy cream
- ✓ 1 cup whole milk
- ✓ 3/4 cup granulated sugar
- ✓ 1 vanilla bean, split, and seeds scraped (or 2 teaspoons pure vanilla extract)
- ✓ 6 large egg yolks
- ✓ Wood chips for smoking (e.g., hickory or oak)

Method:

1. Preheat your smoker to 225°F (110°C) using the wood chips you choose for smoke flavor.
2. In a saucepan, combine the heavy cream, whole milk, granulated sugar, and scraped seeds from the split vanilla bean.
3. Heat the mixture over medium heat, stirring constantly, until it reaches a gentle simmer. Remove from heat.
4. In a separate bowl, whisk the egg yolks until smooth.
5. Gradually pour the hot cream mixture into the whisked egg yolks, stirring constantly to temper the eggs.

6. Return the mixture to the saucepan and cook over low heat, stirring continuously, until it thickens and coats the back of a spoon (about 5-7 minutes). Do not let it boil.
7. Remove the mixture from heat and let it cool to room temperature.
8. Once cooled, strain the mixture through a fine-mesh sieve into a clean bowl to remove the vanilla bean remnants.
9. Transfer the mixture to an ice cream maker and churn according to the manufacturer's instructions.
10. Place the ice cream maker on the smoker grate while churning. Allow the smoke to infuse the ice cream during churning for approximately 20-30 minutes.
11. Once the ice cream reaches a firm but scoopable consistency, transfer it to an airtight container and freeze it for a few hours or until it's fully set.
12. Serve the smoked vanilla bean ice cream as a creamy and smoky dessert. Enjoy the unique combination of vanilla and smokiness!

Smoked Espresso Tiramisu

Smoked Espresso Tiramisu is a sophisticated, smoky dessert that coffee lovers will adore. The combination of espresso and smokiness adds depth of flavor to this classic Italian treat.

Prep Time:30 minutes

Ingredients:

- ✓ 6 large egg yolks
- ✓ 3/4 cup granulated sugar
- ✓ 1 cup mascarpone cheese
- ✓ 1 1/2 cups heavy cream
- ✓ 2 cups strong brewed espresso, cooled
- ✓ 1/4 cup coffee liqueur (optional)
- ✓ 24 to 30 ladyfinger cookies
- ✓ Unsweetened cocoa powder for dusting
- ✓ Wood chips for smoking (e.g., hickory or oak)

Method:

1. Preheat your smoker to 225°F (110°C) using the wood chips you choose for smoke flavor.
2. Whisk the large egg yolks and granulated sugar in a heatproof bowl until the mixture is pale and slightly thickened.
3. Place the bowl over a pot of simmering water (double boiler) and whisk constantly until the mixture reaches a temperature of 160°F (71°C) and thickens (about 5-7 minutes).

4. Remove the bowl from heat and let it cool to room temperature.
5. In a separate bowl, whisk the mascarpone cheese until smooth.
6. Gently fold the mascarpone cheese into the egg yolk mixture until well combined.
7. Whip the heavy cream in another bowl until stiff peaks form.
8. Fold the whipped cream into the mascarpone mixture until you have a smooth and airy mixture.
9. In a shallow dish, combine the brewed espresso and coffee liqueur (if using).
10. Quickly dip each ladyfinger into the espresso mixture, ensuring they are moistened but not soggy. Arrange a layer of dipped ladyfingers in the bottom of a serving dish.
11. Spread half of the mascarpone mixture over the ladyfingers.
12. Repeat with another layer of dipped ladyfingers and the remaining mascarpone mixture.
13. Place the serving dish on the smoker grate.
14. Smoke the tiramisu for approximately 30-40 minutes or until it has absorbed a subtle smoky flavor.
15. Remove the smoked espresso tiramisu from the smoker and refrigerate for at least 4 hours or overnight to allow the flavors to meld.
16. Before serving, dust the top with unsweetened cocoa powder.

17. Serve the smoked espresso tiramisu as a sophisticated and smoky dessert. Enjoy the rich coffee and smoky flavors!

Smoked Bourbon Pecan Pie

Smoked Bourbon Pecan Pie is a rich, smoky dessert with a Southern twist. The combination of pecans, bourbon, and a hint of smokiness makes it a flavorful and indulgent treat.

Prep Time:15 minutes

Ingredients:

- ✓ 1 refrigerated pie crust (or homemade if preferred)
- ✓ 2 cups pecan halves
- ✓ 3 large eggs
- ✓ 1 cup granulated sugar
- ✓ 1 cup light corn syrup
- ✓ 1/4 cup bourbon
- ✓ 2 tablespoons unsalted butter, melted
- ✓ 1 teaspoon vanilla extract
- ✓ 1/4 teaspoon salt
- ✓ Wood chips for smoking (e.g., hickory or pecan)

Method:

1. Preheat your smoker to 225°F (110°C) using the wood chips you choose for smoke flavor.
2. Place the pecan halves on a baking sheet and toast them on the smoker grate for 10-15 minutes or until they are lightly toasted and have a smoky aroma. Stir occasionally for even toasting.
3. Roll out the pie crust and fit it into a 9-inch pie dish. Trim any excess crust.

4. In a mixing bowl, whisk the large eggs, granulated sugar, light corn syrup, bourbon, melted unsalted butter, vanilla extract, and salt until well combined.
5. Arrange the toasted pecan halves at the bottom of the pie crust.
6. Pour the bourbon pecan pie filling over the pecans.
7. Place the pie dish on the smoker grate.
8. Smoke the pecan pie for approximately 60-75 minutes or until the filling is set and the crust is golden brown.
9. Remove the smoked bourbon pecan pie from the smoker and let it cool to room temperature.
10. Slice and serve the pie as a rich and smoky dessert. Enjoy the pecan, bourbon, and smoky goodness!

Smoked Raspberry Cheesecake

Smoked Raspberry Cheesecake is a creamy and fruity dessert with a smoky twist. The combination of raspberry swirls and a subtle smokiness makes it a delightful treat for cheesecake lovers.

Prep Time:30 minutes

Ingredients:

- ✓ 1 1/2 cups graham cracker crumbs
- ✓ 1/2 cup unsalted butter, melted
- ✓ 3 (8-ounce) packages of cream cheese, softened
- ✓ 1 cup granulated sugar
- ✓ 3 large eggs
- ✓ 1 teaspoon vanilla extract
- ✓ 1/2 cup sour cream
- ✓ 1/2 cup raspberry preserves or puree
- ✓ Wood chips for smoking (e.g., cherry or applewood)

Method:

1. Preheat your smoker to 225°F (110°C) using the wood chips you choose for smoke flavor.
2. Combine the graham cracker crumbs and melted unsalted butter in a mixing bowl. Press the mixture into the bottom of a 9-inch springform pan to create the crust.
3. In a separate mixing bowl, beat the softened cream cheese and granulated sugar until smooth and creamy.

4. Add the large eggs, one at a time, beating well after each addition.
5. Stir in the vanilla extract and sour cream until the cheesecake filling is well combined.
6. Pour the cheesecake filling over the graham cracker crust in the springform pan.
7. Warm the raspberry preserves or puree slightly and drizzle it over the cheesecake filling.
8. Use a knife or skewer to create swirls by gently dragging it through the raspberry preserves.
9. Place the springform pan on the smoker grate.
10. Smoke the raspberry cheesecake for approximately 60-75 minutes or until the edges are set but the center is slightly jiggly.
11. Remove the smoked raspberry cheesecake from the smoker and let it cool to room temperature.
12. Refrigerate the cheesecake for at least 4 hours or overnight to allow it to set completely.
13. Slice and serve the cheesecake as a creamy and smoky dessert. Enjoy the raspberry swirls and smoky goodness!

Printed in Great Britain
by Amazon

41255814R00059